WHO IS MY NEIGHBOR?

The Salvadorans

Tana Reiff

A Pacemaker® **HOPES** *and* **DREAMS 2** Book

FEARON/JANUS/QUERCUS
Belmont, California

Simon & Schuster Supplementary Education Group

HOPES *and* DREAMS 2

Cover photo: Reuters/BETTMAN News Photos
Cover Design: Rucker Huggins
Illustration: Duane Bibby

ISBN 0–8224–3809–7
Library of Congress Catalog Card Number: 92–71060

Printed in the United States of America
1. 9 8 7 6 5 4 3 2 1
MA

CONTENTS

1 Archbishop Romero

San Salvador, El Salvador,
Central America, 1980

Oscar Romero,
Archbishop of San Salvador,
had much more than Mass
to say today.
The people sitting in church
and listening to the radio
hung onto his every word.

"I speak to the members
of the army and the police,"
Archbishop Romero began.
"Each one of you
is one of us.
We are all the same people.
The peasants you kill
are your own brothers and sisters.
Remember instead the voice of God:
'Thou shalt not kill.'
God's law must win.

In the name of God,
I beg you,
stop the war!"*

Then, all of a sudden,
from the back of the church,
someone fired a gun
at Archbishop Romero.
He fell to the floor,
shot in the heart.
His blood turned
his white robes red.
He died on the spot.

Word of the Archbishop's death
went out all over El Salvador.
Even Ramon and Pilar Samoya
heard about the shooting
in their little village
near the city of San Miguel.

*Adapted from actual words of Oscar
 Arnulfo Romero, Archbishop of San
 Salvador, in his radio sermon on
 March 23, 1980, the day before his death.

The Samoyas were *campesinos,*
or peasants.
Ramon farmed
a little piece of land.
There he grew corn
like the other peasants
who lived in the village.
Pilar took care
of their two small children.
She carried
big jugs of water
up the mountain
from the stream.
She ground up the corn
to make flour.
She cooked
the family's food
on a round iron pan
over burning wood.
The young Samoya family
worked very hard.
Still, they were very poor.

Ramon and Pilar
had heard Archbishop Romero

over the radio.
They had been surprised
to hear his strong words
against the new government
in El Salvador.
They had also heard
about the killing
that was going on
all over their country.

"Archbishop Romero was right
to call for an end
to the killing,"
Ramon said.
"It is time for peace."

"Are we safe
here in our village?"
Pilar asked her husband.

"No one is safe,"
said Ramon.
"All we do is farm
and try to stay alive.
But there has been trouble
even in villages like ours."

"I have heard
of very bad things
that can happen to people,"
said Pilar.
"And some people
have just disappeared!"

"People say 'disappeared,' "
said Ramon.
"But it means 'dead.' "

"I see,"
said Pilar.

"The government
is the army, you know,"
Ramon went on.
"They also have
'death squads'
that they send out
to kill people.
And the government
is not the only problem.
The guerillas
are against the government.
They hurt and kill people, too."

"Is it safe for us
to talk about this?"
asked Pilar.

"I don't know,"
said Ramon.
"We should watch our words.
I only hope
that some good will come
from Archbishop Romero's death.
Maybe now the world
will hear about what's going on
in El Salvador!"

Thinking It Over

1. What do you know
   about the problems
   in El Salvador
   during the 1980s?

2. Are you free
   to "speak your mind"
   at any time?

3. Do you know anyone
   from El Salvador?
   What is that person's story?

4. What language do you suppose
   Ramon and Pilar speak?

2 Screams in the Night

Over the next few months,
Ramon and Pilar
heard more stories
about trouble in other villages.
They heard about death squads
coming into villages
and killing people.
Such stories
never came on the radio.
But word got around
from person to person,
from village to village.

People were being killed
for different reasons.
In some towns and villages,
guerilla forces came in
to keep the government away.
Then the police
or even a death squad

would show up
to fight the guerillas.
Whole villages were burned.
Many people were killed.
In some towns and villages,
people were killed
for speaking out
against the government.
Villages were burned
to the ground
for what seemed
like no reason at all.
This was war.

One night,
as the Samoya family slept,
Pilar heard a scream.
In a second,
she was wide awake.
She heard another scream,
and then another.
The screams were coming
from the house next door.
Then Pilar heard
a shot being fired,

and a second.
After the second shot,
the screams stopped.

"Ramon! Ramon!"
Pilar cried,
shaking her husband's arm.
"Did you hear that?"

"What's going on?"
Ramon asked.

"It's next door,"
said Pilar.
"I think someone's been shot!"

Ramon went to the window.
"I don't see anything,
but I hear
our neighbor Felipe crying!"

Then Ramon and Pilar
both heard a man's voice.
It was not Felipe.
"You, *campesino*!"

came the voice.
"You come along with us!"

"No, no!"
begged Felipe.

"They're dragging Felipe out!"
said Ramon.
"Why? Why?
And look!
Now the house is on fire!"

These little village houses
were built of wood and mud.
The neighbors' house
was a ball of fire
in no time at all.

Pilar cried and cried.
"We are just simple *campesinos*.
Why must they do such things
to people like us?"

"I have no idea
why they came to get Felipe,"

said Ramon.
"He might have been working
for the wrong people.
Or maybe he did nothing at all.
I only wish
we could have helped our neighbor.
Now we must get out of here
and make sure the fire
doesn't get our house, too."

Thinking It Over

1. There is a saying,
   "All's fair in love and war."
   Do you believe this?
   Why or why not?

2. Why are there wars
   between two groups
   in the same country?

3. Why do free countries
   let people say
   what they want?

3 All for the Land

There was nothing left
of Felipe's home.
His wife was dead,
and Felipe had "disappeared."
Neither he nor his body
was ever found.

Ramon looked
at the burned wood
on the ground.
"So this is how
a death squad works,"
he said sadly.
He and some other men
dug a grave
for the burned bones
of Felipe's wife.
"Thank God
they didn't get us all,"
Ramon said.

Village life carried on.
Things seemed safe.
But a short time later,
word came to the people
that their land
would be taken over.
The *campesinos*
got together one night
for a meeting.

"We have always farmed,"
said one man.
"What will we do now?"

"We can do
one of three things,"
another man spoke up.
"We can go to another place
and do farm work for someone else.
We can go to the city
and find work in a factory.
Or, we can join the army."

"None of these ideas
is the answer,"

said Ramon.
"Can you spend your life
picking coffee beans
for the rich people?
Should you go to the city
where there is not enough work
for all the *campesinos*?
Do you want
to join the army
so you can go out
and kill other Salvadorans?"

"But what can we do?"
one man asked.

"We can try to keep our land,"
said Ramon.

"Someone will come
and kill us all
if we stay here!"
said the other man.

"Then so be it!"
shouted Ramon.
As soon as those words

left his mouth,
he felt afraid.
What if the wrong people
found out he had said that?
He sat back down
on a mat on the ground
and said nothing else.

Over the next few weeks,
people began to leave the village.
Some went to big farms
to ask for work.
Some went to the city
to look for factory jobs.
Many of the young men
signed up for the army.
Some stayed in the village.

Ramon and Pilar Samoya
and their two children stayed.
But one day Ramon did something
he never dreamed of doing.
He and some other *campesinos*
went up to San Salvador
to march against the government.
"We cannot let anyone

take our land!"
he told Pilar.

As soon as Ramon
got to San Salvador,
he became afraid
that he had done
the wrong thing.
But the *campesinos* marched
and no one shot at them.
However, Ramon did see someone
taking his picture.
He believed at the time
that it was someone
from the press.

A few days later,
some guerillas came
to Ramon's house.
They wore masks
and carried machine guns.
"You must join us,"
they said.
"We will help you
keep your land."

"I don't want to join,"
said Ramon.
"I don't want to be
on either side of the war.
I just want my land."

The guerillas
tried to take Ramon away.
Ramon kept on saying
he would not fight
on either side.
The guerillas grabbed Ramon,
but he pulled himself free.

As the guerillas
began to leave,
one of them said,
"Think it over well."

"I think I'm in big trouble,"
Ramon told Pilar.
"All I want is to farm
this little piece of land.
Is that too much to ask?"

Thinking It Over

1. If you lived in this village
   and learned that your land
   would be taken over,
   what would you do?

2. If you were Ramon,
   would you have marched
   against the government?
   Why or why not?
   Would you be willing
   to take big chances
   in the name of freedom?

3. What can happen
   to everyday people like Ramon
   if they get caught
   between two sides
   in a civil war?

4 Get Out or Die

A few days after
the guerillas' visit,
Ramon was walking back
from his cornfields.
Five soldiers stopped him
along the open road.
They held long guns,
pointed toward the sky.
One of the soldiers
pulled from his pocket
a picture of Ramon
from his day in San Salvador.
"Are you Ramon Samoya?"
asked the soldier.
"Are you working
for the guerillas?"

"I am not on either side.
Please don't kill me,"
Ramon begged.

"Lie down on the road,"
said the soldier.
He pushed Ramon's face
into the hot road
and pointed his gun
at Ramon's head.

"Are you ready to talk,
or do you want to die?"
the soldier asked Ramon.

"You will have to kill me,"
said Ramon.
"What do you want me to say?"

Just then, an old man
came along on the road.
"Stop!" called the old man.
"That is Ramon Samoya.
He is not working for the guerillas.
He is a hard-working *campesino,*
nothing else.
Don't kill him."

"Who are you?"
one soldier asked the old man.

"I was his teacher
when he was a young boy.
I have known Ramon
all his life.
He has nothing to do
with the guerillas."

The soldier let go
of Ramon's head.
"Today you may go free,"
said the soldier.
"But if you know
what is good for you,
you will leave your land.
If you stay here,
we will kill
you and your family
and we will give your bones
back to the earth!"
With that,
the soldier kicked Ramon
in the head.

Ramon walked back
to the village.
There was blood from his head

all over him.
"I must leave here
as soon as possible,"
he told Pilar.
"It's the only way."

"Will the children and I
go with you?"
Pilar asked.

"You must stay here,"
said Ramon.
"The trip will be too hard
for you and the children.
I don't think
anyone will hurt you
if I leave as I was told to.
I will be back
as soon as things cool off."

Then he stayed up all night,
thinking about what to do next.

Thinking It Over

1. Have you ever been in trouble
   when someone came along
   to save you
   at just the right time?

2. If you were Ramon,
   would you have left
   your family behind?
   Why or why not?

3. What do you think
   Ramon will do next?

5 Leaving the Country

Ramon put some things
into a small bag
and walked to San Miguel.
There, he got a visa
to visit Mexico.
A few days later,
he boarded a bus
headed north to Guatemala
and then into Mexico.
From there,
he hoped to cross the border
into the United States,
even without papers.

It would be
a very long way to go.
Ramon, the *campesino* corn farmer,
had never been out of El Salvador.
He was afraid.
He knew he would not be safe
without papers in a different country.

But he would be less safe
as a man marked for death
in his own country.

  Ramon sat in the bus
and looked out the window.
He saw the beautiful green land
and high mountains
of El Salvador.
The bus passed large areas
of burned houses and trees
that once were villages.
Here and there were soldiers
stationed along the road.
"Why must they fight
over this beautiful country?"
he said to himself.

  The miles passed,
one by one.
Ramon changed buses
three or four times
along the way.
With each new bus,
he knew he had moved
so many more miles

away from Pilar and the children.
He worried about them
every minute.

At the border of Mexico,
the bus had to stop.
All the people
had to be checked
before they could go into Mexico.
Ramon showed his visa.
He passed the check.
But some of the people
had no papers at all.
Ramon saw some of them
giving money to the Border Patrol.
The people who had
no papers and no money
had to get off the bus
and go with the Border Patrol men.
Ramon wondered
what would happen to these people.

The bus went on.
Days later,
Ramon found himself
all the way up

in the north of Mexico.
He was too close
to the United States
to ride the bus anymore.
Besides, he was out of money.

He walked the back roads.
Once or twice a day,
he would stop at a house
to beg for food.
But he was still hungry
most of the time,
and he was very tired.
When he reached the Rio Grande,
it was getting dark.
On the other side of the river
was the United States.

Ramon took off his shoes
and put them into his bag.
He tied the bag
onto his back.
Then, when he was sure
that no one was looking,
he made the sign of the cross
and began to swim.

The Rio Grande isn't very wide.
Ramon was able to swim
across the river
in a few minutes.
As he got close
to the other side,
he spotted some people
standing near the water.
He ducked under water
and tried to swim
to another landing point.

Ramon swam and swam.
When he was too tired
to go any farther,
he headed toward the river bank.
His legs were weak
as he tried to stand up.

Just then,
two men came running up.
They each grabbed
one of Ramon's arms
and cuffed his hands
behind his back.
The long, hard trip was over.

Thinking It Over

1. If you were going on a trip
   and could take
   only one small bag,
   what would you put in it?

2. If you were Ramon,
   would you have tried this trip
   all by yourself?

3. Why do people like Ramon
   try doing things
   like swimming
   across the Rio Grande?

4. What do you think
   the men will do with Ramon?

6 Back Again

The Border Patrol people
put Ramon in jail.
"Please don't send me
back to El Salvador,"
Ramon begged.
"My family and I
will be killed!"

"That's what they all say!"
laughed the men at the jail.

"But, really, we will!"
cried Ramon.

It was a waste of time.
The whole trip
had been a waste.
A paper written in English
was put before Ramon.
He signed his name
without knowing what it was.

Before he knew it,
Ramon was on his way
back to El Salvador.

He was sent to San Salvador.
From there,
he wasn't sure
if he should go back
to his village.
But he couldn't stay away.
He had to see
if his family was all right.

Ramon walked most of the way.
As he got near,
he saw that his worries
were all real.
The village was gone.
All the little houses
were burned to the ground.
All the cornfields
were burned to the ground.
Dead bodies were all over.

He found the place
where his house had been.

He looked for the bodies
of his family.
He saw the iron pan
that Pilar always cooked on.
But he saw nothing
that looked like a body.
He sat down
in the mess
that was once his home.
He wanted to die,
and he felt too tired
even to cry.
What could have happened
to his loved ones?
He didn't want to think
of the horrible end
they must have come to.
Yet all kinds of dark pictures
danced in his mind
and would not go away.

Ramon did the only thing
he could think of doing.
He left right away
and headed for Mexico
all over again.

    This time, however,
he decided to make some money.
He would need to pay a *coyote*,
a person who could take him
into the United States.
When he reached Mexico City,
he found jobs
that did not need work papers.
He saved up 400 dollars.
It was enough to pay a *coyote*
for a bus ride
into the United States.
It was not enough
to get Ramon to a safe house,
or to buy any false papers.
It was only enough
to get him across the border.

    Ramon found out
where to meet the *coyote*.
A small crowd of people
all found the place.
"There must be 40 people here,"
Ramon said to himself.
"It must be a big bus
to fit all these people."

The bus was not big.
In fact, it was a very small bus.
It had no seats.
The people just packed in.
There were no windows,
and it was hard to get air.
And with each passing hour,
the bus grew hotter.
"Now, Lord,"
said Ramon.
"Let me die now."

The day passed
and then the night.
The next morning,
the *coyote* told the people
they were almost in Arizona.
Ramon felt a little better
to think he was almost safe
in the United States.
He would not have to
cross the river
into Texas this time.
The *coyote* would go by land
right into Arizona.

The bus crossed the border
with no trouble.
Tired, hot, and hungry as they were,
everyone on the bus
let out a cry of joy.

The bus went on
for another ten miles or so
before coming to a stop.
Then the *coyote* said,
"OK, everyone off!"

The back door opened,
and one by one
the people jumped out.
As soon as everyone was out,
the bus pulled away.
They were on their own now.

Ramon looked around.
The *coyote* had left the people
in the Arizona desert.

Thinking It Over

1. Why do you think
   Ramon's village was burned?

2. From what you know about them,
   what do you think
   of the way many *coyotes* work?

3. Why do people trust people
   like the *coyote* in this story?

7 In a Bad Fix

"What do we do now?"
asked one woman,
who found it hard to talk.
Like the others,
she needed something to drink.

It was early morning,
and the air was cool.
It felt good.
But this was the desert.
As the people sat and waited,
the sun rose higher
and the air grew hotter.
There was no water around,
only a cactus here or there.

"Does anyone know
how to get juice
out of a cactus?"
someone asked.

Ramon walked over
to a tall cactus.
He reached out
to see if the plant's spines
were too sharp to touch.
Just like that,
an inch-long spine
stuck deep in his hand.
"Ouch!" he cried.
He tried to pull it out
and it stuck in his finger, too.
Another man sat down
under a cactus
to get away from the sun.
He got sharp spines
stuck all over his back.
The people gave up
on trying to get cactus juice.

Some of the women began to pray.
Two of the older women
didn't live to see the night.
The bus ride and the desert
had been too much for them.
The next morning,
the heat started all over again.

The people took off
most of their clothes
to try to keep cool.
It didn't help much.
By noon,
everyone was down on the sand.
They were all half dead.
Then Ramon heard the noise
of an engine.
When he first spotted the van
coming toward the group,
he believed it was
only in his mind.
But when two young nuns
got out and handed him water,
he knew it was real.

"Come with us,"
said one of the nuns.
"We will take you to a safe place."

The people packed into the van.
It was more crowded
than the *coyote*'s bus.
But they believed the nuns
when they said that everyone

would soon be safe.
And as they drove on,
the nuns gave out food and water.

They came to a house
in a small town.
The nuns helped the people
walk inside.
There, they found other Salvadorans
and some Guatemalans, too.

"We are a safe house
for Central American refugees,"
said Sister Dora in Spanish.
"We will nurse you back to health.
When you are well enough,
we will help you go
to other safe houses."

"I have no papers,"
said Ramon.

The nun smiled.
"We understand that,"
she said softly.
"That's why you need help."

Thinking It Over

1. What kinds of things
   do people do
   to stay alive
   in a bad fix?

2. Do you believe
   people like Ramon
   should be let into the country?
   Why or why not?

3. Do you think nuns
   (or anyone else)
   should help people
   who come into the country
   without papers?
   Why or why not?

8 Sanctuary

Ramon was in bad shape.
He was very weak and dirty.
Most of all, he needed water.
He needed good food, too,
because he had not been eating well
for a long time.
A doctor gave him something
to clear up his skin and eyes.
He got all cleaned up,
and the nuns gave him fresh clothes.

"Thank you, thank you,"
Ramon told the nuns.
"Why do you do this for us?"

"We answer a need,"
said Sister Dora.

"But you don't even know us,"
said Ramon.

"The Bible says
to love your neighbor as yourself,"
said Sister Dora.
"You are our neighbor."

"Back in El Salvador,
I don't know *who* is my neighbor,"
said Ramon.
"You don't know
who is from the government
and who is a guerilla.
You can't trust anyone.
The guerillas wanted me
to join them,
and the army told me
that I would be killed
if I didn't get out of the country.
So here I am,
on my second try.
I made it.
I am one of the lucky ones."

"We know it is very hard
for you Central Americans,"
said Sister Dora.

"Can you get me papers
to stay in the United States?"
Ramon asked the nun.

"We would if we could,"
said Sister Dora.
"But you might as well
not even apply for asylum."

"What's *asylum*?"
Ramon wondered.

"Asylum would let you stay
in the United States
because you are not safe
in your home country,"
said Sister Dora.
"But Salvadorans
are just not being granted asylum.
Even if you show up to apply,
you are taking a chance
of being sent back.
Our government says
you only came here
to work and make money."

"I came here to *live,*"
said Ramon.
"Back there I would be dead.
I think they got my wife already."

"That is very sad,"
said Sister Dora.
"I feel for your pain."

A few weeks later,
Sister Dora told Ramon
he would be going to Texas
on a bus.
"A family in Texas
will keep you in their home,"
Sister Dora explained.
"One of them will meet you
at the bus station."

"Isn't that family
taking a big chance?"
asked Ramon.

"Yes, they are,"
said Sister Dora.

"They risk jail time and a big fine.
But they feel that God's law
is greater than man's.
They feel they are right
in the eyes of God.
They will give you sanctuary."

"What is *sanctuary*?"
asked Ramon.

"Sanctuary means a safe place,"
Sister Dora explained.
"People who give sanctuary
take you in
and help keep you safe."

The bus came to a stop
in a small town in Texas.
An American named Barney Fuller
met Ramon at the little station.
Barney spoke a little Spanish,
but not much.
Ramon couldn't understand
everything Barney said.
Barney couldn't understand
everything Ramon said.

But the two men
got across to each other
as well as they could.

At first it was very strange
for Ramon to live
in this American home.
He was, after all,
a *campesino* from El Salvador.
He had never had running water
right out of the tap.
He had never had a kitchen,
or a soft bed with sheets.
He had never seen
all the kinds of food
that Sarah Fuller
put on the table.
There was a lot to get used to.

What's more,
Ramon did not always feel well.
If he began to think
about what had happened to him,
he would shake all over.
He had trouble sleeping
and had many bad dreams.

His body had gotten well,
but his mind still hurt.

The Fullers helped Ramon
find work as a clean-up man
at a big restaurant
where he could get lost
in the crowd.
Ramon helped out
around the Fullers' house
in any way he could.
He went to church with them
every Sunday morning.
Still, he felt in his heart
that he could not live like this
for very long.
As kind as the Fullers were,
Ramon didn't feel
as if he belonged here.
But he stayed,
because there was no other place
for him to go right now.
He felt lucky
to be right where he was.
Living "underground"
was better than not living at all.

Thinking It Over

1. Who is your neighbor?

2. Do you know
   why the U.S. government
   took the stand it did
   toward Salvadoran refugees
   during the 1980s?

3. What does it mean
   to live "underground"?

9 Lost and Found

Ramon missed his family.
Some days,
Pilar and the children
were all he could think about.
Sometimes, the sound of his mop
pushing back and forth
across the restaurant floor
seemed to be saying,
"Pilar, Pilar, Pilar."

Then one night,
when he came back from work,
Sarah Fuller said,
"Sit down, Ramon.
We need to tell you
about something interesting."

Ramon sat down.

"We got a phone call today,"
Sarah began.

"A church in Houston, Texas,
is helping a Salvadoran woman
and her two children.
Her name is Pilar.
Wasn't that your wife's name?"

"Yes," said Ramon.
His heart began to beat fast.

"The people in Houston
seem to believe
their Pilar may be your wife,"
said Sarah.
"They tracked you down
with the help of the nuns
in Arizona.
Now did your Pilar
use the last name of Mendez?"

Ramon's heart began to sink.
"No," he said.
"She was Pilar Samoya.
She used my last name.
I guess this woman
is not my wife.
My wife is dead after all."

"Maybe and maybe not,"
said Sarah.
"Many Central Americans
are afraid to use their real names
if they come here
with no papers.
They use a different name
to try to stay out of trouble."

Ramon's heart lifted again.

"The woman I spoke with
is sending us a picture
of this Pilar and her children,"
Sarah went on.
"We should know for sure
who she is
in a day or two."

There was nothing from Houston
in the next day's mail.
But the day after that,
something did come
from the church in Houston.
Sarah Fuller let Ramon
open the mail.

Ramon tore it open
as fast as he could.
He pulled out the picture
that was inside.
He looked at it
for only a second.
"It's my Pilar!"
he cried.
"She is alive!
She is alive!
And the children too!"

Sarah and Barney Fuller
cried for joy with Ramon.

"I must go to Houston,"
said Ramon.
"I thank you
for all you have done for me.
But I must go to my wife."

The next morning,
Ramon was packed
and ready to leave.
He said his good-byes
to Sarah and the Fuller children.

Then Barney drove Ramon
to the bus station.
"You be careful,"
Barney told him
as the bus pulled away
from the station.

Two hours later,
the bus pulled into Houston.
This time,
the face that met Ramon
at the station
was one he knew well.
It was Pilar,
a little older and a bit worn,
but alive and well
in Houston, Texas.

Thinking It Over

1. Have you ever tried
   to "track someone down"—
   to find someone?
   How did you—
   or would you—do it?

2. Are you part of a group
   that helps people in some way?
   What do you do?

3. How do you think
   Pilar was able
   to get out of El Salvador?

10 City Life

"What happened to you?"
Ramon asked Pilar.
"I went back to the village
and everything was burned.
I couldn't find you
or your bones.
I had every reason to believe
that they took you away
and you 'disappeared.' "

"The village was burned?"
Pilar asked.
"I didn't know that.
After you left
some men came looking for you.
I don't know
if they were guerillas or the army.
They wanted me to tell them
where you went.
Of course,
I didn't know.

So they beat me up.
After that happened,
I decided I had to leave, too.
There was no way
I could get in touch with you.
So I took the children
and we headed north."

"Where did you go?"
Ramon asked.

"We spent a long time
in a refugee camp in Honduras
called Mesa Grande,"
Pilar explained.
She told about how they lived
in a long building
with a tin roof.
The camp had
so many buildings like this
that Pilar couldn't count them all.
The air was hot and heavy
and smelled like sick people.
Children played
in dirty water.
There was never enough food

for the 10,000 people there.
Many people died.

"But we were lucky,"
said Pilar.
"We are young and strong
and we made it.
We got to the United States
only by the will of God."

"How did you come
into this country?
How did you cross the border?"
Ramon wanted to know.

"We left the camp
and got ourselves onto a train,"
said Pilar.
"We had no money.
We had to hide in a box car.
We got over the border,
but we were caught right away.
Then some nice people
posted bonds for us
and got us out
of the detention camp

before we could be sent home.
We have been in Houston
ever since."

"I am so sorry
that you had a hard time,"
said Ramon.
"But we are together now.
We are very, very lucky."

The Houston church
helped Ramon and Pilar Samoya
get an apartment of their own.
Ramon found another job
in a restaurant.
Pilar stayed home with the children,
because she was afraid
to send them to school.
She was afraid
someone would find out
that the family
did not have papers.
The people from the church
believed that the children
were in school,
but they were not.

Then Ramon found out
that the highest court
had ruled that children
should go to school,
even if their parents
did not have papers.
So the Samoya children
began going to school.
It was very hard for them
because they spoke little English.
They missed many days.
Some of the other children
picked fights with them
and called them "wetbacks."

Ramon understood
how hard this was for the children.
City life was hard for him, too.
But he told the children
they had to go to school.
He wanted them to learn,
and the law said they had to go.
And so they went.

The children brought home
many new English words.

Ramon and Pilar
picked up some English
from their children.

"We don't know
how long we will be here,"
said Ramon.
"It won't hurt
to know some English."

But all during these years,
the Samoya family
was always afraid.
If they were ever found out,
they would be sent back
to El Salvador.
Their names might go on a list
that would be sent
to the wrong people.
Living in Houston felt safer
than living in El Salvador.
But not for a minute
did Ramon and Pilar Samoya
feel as safe
as they wished they could.

Thinking It Over

1. Have you ever known someone
   who didn't have papers?
   How did he or she get by?

2. Why do you think it is law
   that all children
   must go to school?

3. Do you feel safe
   in the way you live?
   Why or why not?
   What makes you feel safe?

11 Asylum

A month didn't go by
that Ramon and Pilar
didn't hear a story
about other Salvadorans.
They had a television now,
and they saw the war
in El Salvador
right in their living room.
They saw news about the trouble
Salvadorans were still having
as they tried to come
to the United States.
They met other Central Americans
who were living "underground"
just like they were.

"My heart goes out
to these people,"
said Ramon one night.
"I don't even know all the people
who live in this apartment building.

But the Central Americans
that we hear about—
these people are our neighbors.
I wish I could help them."

"You are one of them,"
said Pilar.
"People like us
cannot show ourselves
to the world
in any way.
We cannot make any noise."

"We might be able
to go to Canada,"
said Ramon.
"We could get papers up there."

"I think we should stay here,"
said Pilar.
"If the day ever comes
when we can return home,
we are not so far away."

Then one day
a woman from the church

came to see the Samoyas.
"Let's talk about asylum,"
she began.
"We are seeing more Salvadorans
being granted asylum now.
The government is not as tight
about this as it was before,
and you people have a good case.
We would like to help you
apply for asylum,
if you want to try."

Ramon and Pilar
looked at each other.
They were both thinking
how nice it would be
not to be afraid
of being caught and sent back
to El Salvador.

"What if they turn us down?"
Pilar asked.

"They may turn you down,"
said the church woman.
"But they would probably free you

without posting a bond.
Things have changed a bit
since you came here."

"We are ready to try,"
said Ramon.

People from the church
helped Ramon and Pilar
get their case ready.
The main point of their case
was that the guerillas
had tried to force Ramon
to join them.
To the U.S. government,
this was a better reason
for coming to the United States
than just for work.

Filling out papers,
talking to people,
and waiting for something to happen
took close to a year.
Then the news came.
Ramon and Pilar
had been granted asylum!

They could stay in the U.S.
on the grounds
that they were not safe
in their own country.
Ramon was happy
that he and his family could stay.
"But what about all the others?"
he wondered.
"They all left El Salvador
for good reasons."

"What's on your mind, Ramon?"
Pilar asked him.

"I must find a way
to help other Central Americans,"
said Ramon.
"Now I have papers.
Now I can do something.
The question is,
what can I do?"

As he had done
before he left El Salvador,
Ramon stayed up all night,
thinking about what to do.

Thinking It Over

1. If you ran the U.S. government,
   how would you decide
   who gets to stay
   in the country?

2. What makes a person
   feel a need to help others?

3. What are ways
   in which Ramon could help
   his people?

12 Hope for Peace

It was not safe for Ramon
to return to El Salvador.
So he couldn't help Salvadorans
back in his own country.
It was not safe
for him to be in Mexico.
So he couldn't help people
cross the border.
Besides, it was against the law
and could end his asylum.

So Ramon talked with Pilar,
and they began
to take Salvadoran refugees
into their home.
There was word that
the U.S. government might give
"temporary protected status," or TPS,
to Salvadorans as a group.
TPS would let almost everyone
stay in the United States

until the end of the war
in El Salvador.
Until then, people needed help
to stay in the country.

One of the people
who stayed with the Samoyas
was a young woman
whose husband and children
had been killed.
She stayed for a long time.
The Samoyas also kept
a husband and wife
whose home had been burned
because their son
ran away from the army.
This couple stayed until they found
other family members in Los Angeles.

When Ramon
first came to Houston,
he could not read and write.
He went to school and learned
to read and write in English.
Now, a few years later,
he was so good at it

that he began helping people
fill out papers to get TPS.
He was a big help
since he could speak
both Spanish and English.
Ramon also started a self-help group
for Salvadorans and Guatemalans
coming into the United States.
He taught them
how to help themselves
get their lives in order.

Then came the best news of all.
A peace plan for El Salvador
was signed in January 1992
by the government of El Salvador
and the guerillas.
Ramon and Pilar saw on TV
the crowds of happy people
on the streets of San Salvador.
That same day,
Barney and Sarah Fuller called.

"What do you think
of this big news?"
Sarah asked.

"We'll wait and see,"
said Ramon on the phone.

"You sound rather cool.
Aren't you very happy?"
Sarah asked.

"I will be very happy
if the peace plan works,"
said Ramon.
"Five times already
they have tried to end the war.
But this time looks the best."

"What will you do?"
Barney asked.
"Will you go back to El Salvador?"

"I cannot think
about going back
until we are sure
there is no more fighting,
no more death squads,"
said Ramon.
"Besides, our children
are going to good schools

and we have started to build
a better life here.
Maybe we will find a way to stay."

"You are doing great work
with the Central Americans,"
Sarah said.

"They are my neighbors,"
said Ramon.
"Like you and Barney
and the nuns in Arizona and Texas
and all the people
all over the country
who are helping us,
I must help to answer a need.
So for now,
my work is here."

"You never asked for this,
did you, Ramon?"
Barney asked.

"No, no," laughed Ramon.
"I'm just lucky.
And I know it."

Thinking It Over

1. Have you ever helped someone
   who was new in the country?
   If so, how?
   What kinds of help
   do any new people need most?

2. Have you ever been part
   of a self-help group?
   Did it help you
   learn to help yourself?

3. Why would a person like Ramon
   feel he was lucky?